Contents

What Is Mail Fraud?

It's a scheme to get money or something of value from you by offering a product, service, or investment opportunity that does not live up to its claims. Prosecutors must prove the claims were intentionally misrepresented and that the mail was used to carry out the scheme.

Although most mail-order companies are honest and stand behind their products and services, unfortunately there are a few rotten apples who give direct mail advertisers a bad name. They cheat people by peddling worthless products, medical quackery, and get-rich-quick schemes. Some fly-by-nights take your money and send you nothing.

Unscrupulous businesses don't mind taking advantage of an unwary customer. "Let the buyer beware" is their motto — and you might be the buyer.

Mail fraudsters frequently rely on the same old tricks. You may even be familiar with some of them. The following pages include some of the more common mail fraud schemes and related consumer problems. Watch out for them!

Sweepstakes and 'Free' Prizes

It happens every day. Thousands of people are notified by mail that they have won a free prize. Usually, it's a postcard that says your prize will be one of four or five "valuable" items — like a new car, a color television, or a $1,000 savings bond.

Typically, con artists whose sole purpose is to rip you off mail these notices. When you contact the company by phone to claim your prize, the scam artist will tell you that you are required to pay a "processing" or "insurance" fee and pressure you to give out your credit card number. Don't do it! The con artist may make thousands of dollars in unauthorized charges to your account. If you refuse to give out your credit card number, beware of the con artist's other scam — convincing you to cover the processing or insurance fee by sending a check for hundreds of dollars by overnight courier, or by wiring the fee to a person or business in Canada, Costa Rica, or another foreign location.

Either way, you can be certain that your prize will cost you more than it's worth — or it may never arrive at all.

Business Tip: Advertising specialty products like pens, key tags, baseball caps, and ice scrapers, to name a few, has helped many companies gain recognition. However, illegal "boiler room" operations also use these products to ensnare owners and employees of small companies in a fraud scheme.

The scheme begins with a notification that you've won a big prize in a sweepstakes promotion. But there's a catch — you are told that you must purchase a certain quantity of items with your company name and logo to avoid a "gift tax." The purchase, which can amount to several thousand dollars, may result in inferior merchandise or nothing at all.

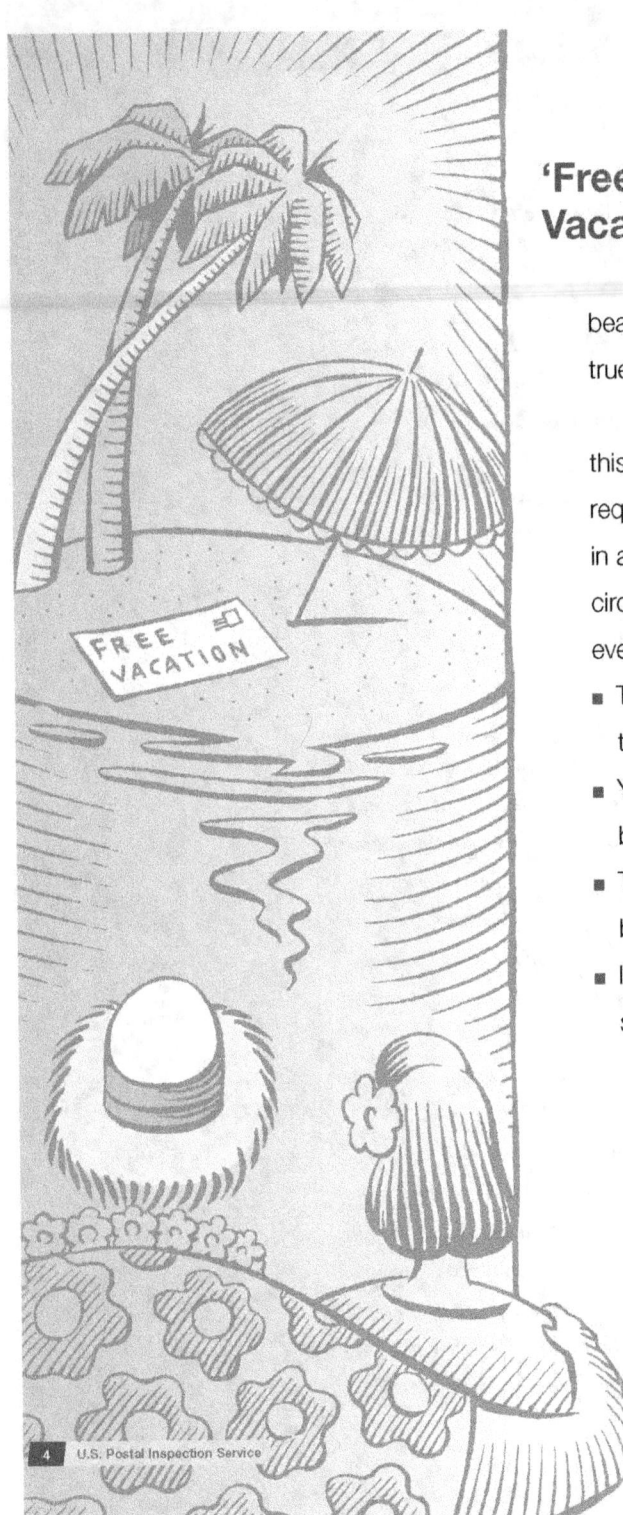

'Free' Vacations

"Congratulations! You have won a free vacation for two in beautiful, sun-drenched Bermuda." Sound too good to be true? It probably is.

There's always a catch. In the most common form of this scam, to be eligible for the free vacation you will either be required to pay a service charge or to purchase a membership in a travel club. Don't pay it. And do not, under any circumstances, give the company your credit card number or even its expiration date. If you do, here's what you can expect:

- There will be many restrictions on when you can take your trip.
- You may be required to pay an additional handling charge to book your reservation.
- The travel dates you prefer will very likely be unavailable.
- If you complain, you may be offered an upgraded plan for still another additional fee.

Government Look-Alike Mail

That brown envelope in your mailbox looked so official you thought it was from a government agency. Even the name, return address, and seal looked official. Such mailings can be deceptive and confusing, and are sometimes illegal. They typically contain sweepstakes solicitations or requests for donations to political causes. Such mailings are no longer allowed unless:

- The entity actually has a government connection, approval, or endorsement.
- The mail and its envelope bear a notice that disclaims such connection, approval, or endorsement by a government agency.
- The material is contained in a publication purchased or requested by the addressee.

Carefully read the material inside the envelope to determine if it really is from a government agency.

Solicitations Disguised As Invoices

Don't be victimized by con artists who try to get you to order goods or services by mailing solicitations that look like invoices. The unscrupulous individuals who mail these know that some unsuspecting individuals will be fooled by their appearance and will automatically pay, thinking they may have placed an order but forgot about it.

Some solicitations disguise their true nature. Others identify themselves as solicitations, but only in the fine print. In either case, withhold payment until you have verified whether you actually ordered and received the goods or services reflected on the document. If not, do not pay. You may have received a solicitation in the guise of an invoice.

Business Tip: Watch out for "Yellow Pages" advertising invoices designed to look like they're from your local telephone directory publisher. You can almost always be assured that these bills are bogus. Charges for genuine Yellow Pages advertising will appear on your local telephone bill.

Foreign Lotteries

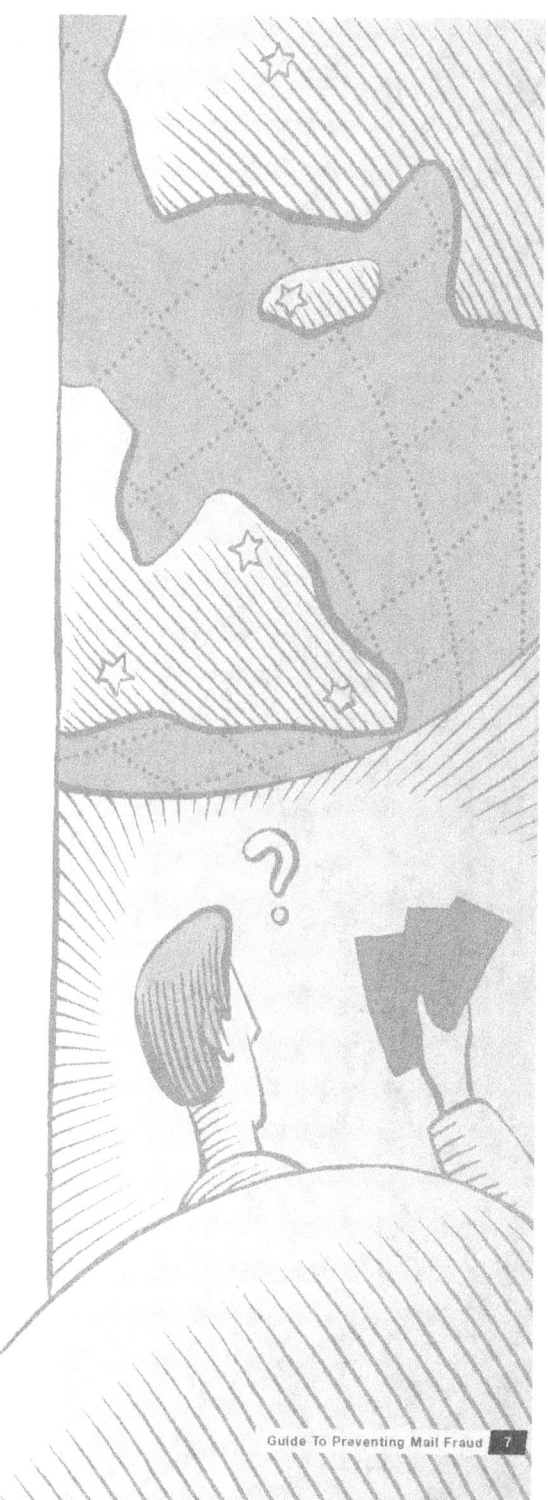

You hear the state lotto jingle on the radio. The jackpot has been raised to $10 million. You've got lotto fever! Next thing you know there's a brochure in your mailbox urging you to participate in some foreign country's lottery — maybe one in Australia or Canada — via the convenient mail-order purchase of lottery tickets, or of a share in a pool of lottery tickets.

We've got a hot tip for you: Don't fall for it! Here's why:

- It's illegal. A federal statute prohibits mailing payments to purchase any ticket, share, or chance in a foreign lottery. Except for state-owned and -operated lotteries, federal law prohibits sending lottery material through the mail.

- It's probably a scam. Most — if not all — foreign lottery come-ons sent to U.S. addresses through the mail are bogus. They don't come from foreign government agencies or licensees. Instead, they come from con artists who take your money and give you nothing in return.

Chain Letters

Have you ever received a chain letter or e-mail message guaranteeing you'll "earn big $$$$" with one small investment? All you have to do is send $10 to everyone on the list, place your name at the bottom of the list, and mail it to 10 friends. Then just sit back and watch the checks fill your mailbox.

Don't waste your money. Chain letters don't work. What's more, if you mail chain letters, you could be committing a federal crime. The same law that prohibits lotteries applies to chain letters as well.

Look at the chart. You can see that more participants are required than there are people in the entire world! The first investor in the chain may receive some money, but later participants rarely get even their original investments back.

No. of Mailings	No. of Participants
1	6
2	36
3	216
4	1,296
5	7,776
6	46,656
7	279,936
8	1,679,616
9	10,077,696
10	60,466,176
11	362,797,056
12	2,176,782,336
13	13,060,694,016

U.S. Population: More Than 300 Million
World Population: More Than 6 Billion

Charity Fraud

Most mail solicitations for charitable contributions are legitimate appeals for a good cause. Some are phony. Charity fraud does a lot of harm. The swindler takes advantage of people's good will and takes their cash — money meant for people in need.

Give to charities you know. Check out the ones you have never heard of, or whose names are similar to well-known charities. Also:

- Be suspicious of charities that accept only cash.
- Always make out your check or money order to the organization to which you want to donate money, not to an individual.

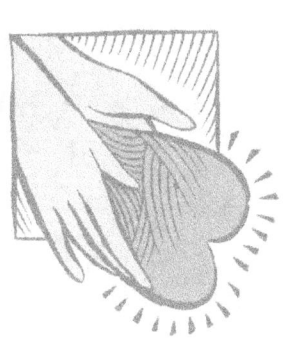

Insurance Fraud

Slick operators who run insurance policy schemes will try to sell you anything in the insurance line, regardless of your existing coverage or need. The premiums far exceed those charged by reputable insurance firms. Watch for these scam-related tricks:

- A request for cash payments.
- A request for lump-sum payments as far as a year in advance.
- An offer of last-chance insurance bargains.
- A request that you sign a blank insurance form.

When purchasing insurance, be sure to read all the fine print on documents and purchase only the insurance coverage you need. Discuss the offer with an attorney or a knowledgeable friend or relative before signing any document.

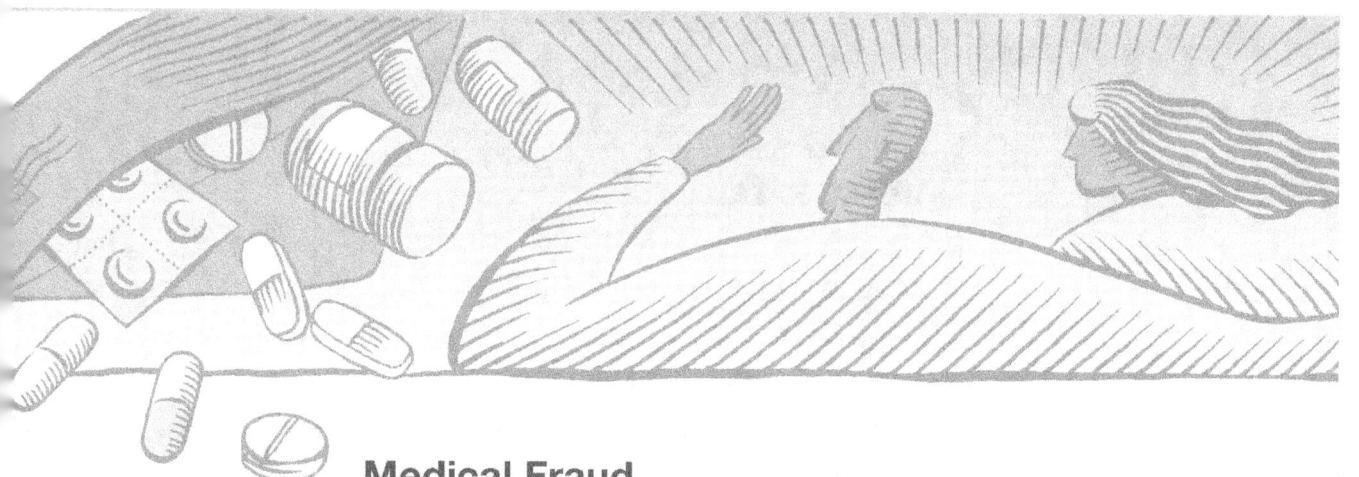

Medical Fraud

For years medical quacks have sold powders, pills, lotions, and other gimmicks through the mail to people seeking cures for baldness, obesity, or sexual dysfunction. Tremendous medical advances have made the successful treatment of such conditions a reality. Despite legitimate medical breakthroughs, snake-oil merchants continue to peddle worthless potions, offering "miracles" like:

- Instant cure for arthritis!
- Lose weight overnight!
- Look years younger!

The gadgets and gimmicks advertised are not tested by competent medical authorities, and some are downright dangerous, so:

- Don't trust your health to a salesperson.
- Don't believe claims of a secret cure or miracle drug. (Such advances make big news worldwide.)
- Be suspicious of claims of excessive weight loss.
- Don't believe exaggerated claims of regained youth or the perfect figure.

Protect your health and your pocketbook. Before purchasing any cure-alls, consult your family physician.

Internet Fraud

The Internet is teeming with fraudulent schemes, and swindlers find it easy to exploit innocent victims online. Fraud on the Internet results in mail fraud when "cyberscammers" receive payments and ship items via the U.S. Mail.

For example, winners of online auctions may never receive the advertised item: After dishonest sellers receive payment, they fail to ship the item. Online crooks use the anonymity offered by the Internet and a rented address at a commercial mail receiving agency to hide their identities. In general, it can be difficult to know with whom you are dealing when conducting business online.

Cyberscammers may also bid on their own auction items, under another user ID, to raise bid amounts. Or they may contact bidders from an auction to inform them that the winner failed to make payment and the item is still available. Again, despite a mailed-in payment, no merchandise is sent. The advantage to con artists using this tactic is that the online auction site is not involved and the victim is unable to seek help with the problem.

Phony Inheritance Schemes

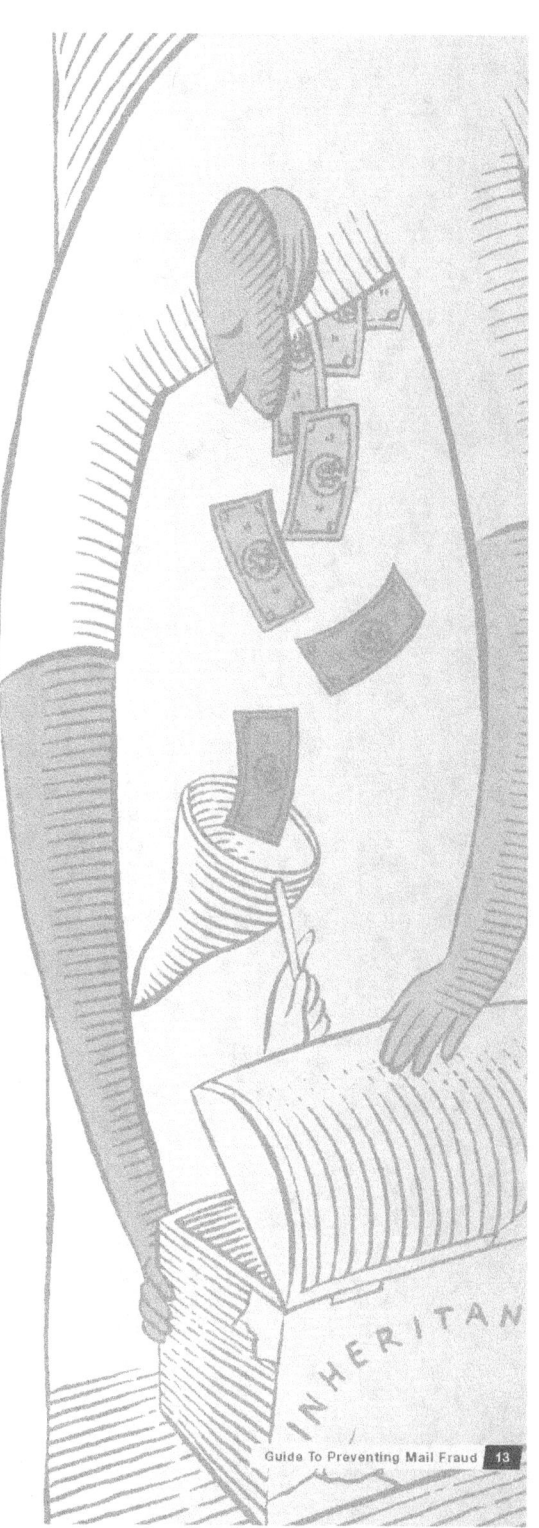

Wouldn't it be nice if you unexpectedly came into an inheritance from a long-lost relative or friend? It rarely happens. If you receive a notification in the mail from an "estate locator" saying that there is an unclaimed inheritance waiting for you, beware! You could be the target of a slick con artist.

These unscrupulous white-collar criminals also call themselves "research specialists" — but they didn't find you by doing research. You are one of thousands across the nation who are targeted in mass mailings. Many of these recipients are lured into mailing a fee — sometimes $30 or more — for an "estate report." All the individuals on the mailing list receive the same information, so chances are almost zero that you are the heir.

You can protect yourself by checking other sources before sending funds in response to an estate-locator solicitation. Those who have been named to distribute estate funds to rightful heirs normally do not request you to pay a fee to find out about your share of the estate.

Home Improvement and Home Repair Fraud

Because home repairs and improvements are expensive, con artists and thieves have entered the industry to rip you off. Be careful if someone mails you a brochure offering to do an expensive job for an unusually low price. Once you sign the contract, you will learn why the price is so low: The firm never delivers the service you paid for in advance.

Free inspections by con artists turn up plenty of expensive repairs you don't need. Some shady operators offer to do the work on the spot. However, when they leave, you may be left with a large bill and a faulty repair job. Here are some precautions you can take to make an informed decision:

- Always get several estimates for every repair job.
- Verify the company's name and address.
- Ask for references and check them out.
- Contact your local Better Business Bureau to check the company's reputation before you authorize work or pay any money.
- Make sure you understand the details of a contract before you sign.
- Inspect the finished product before you pay, and never pay in cash.

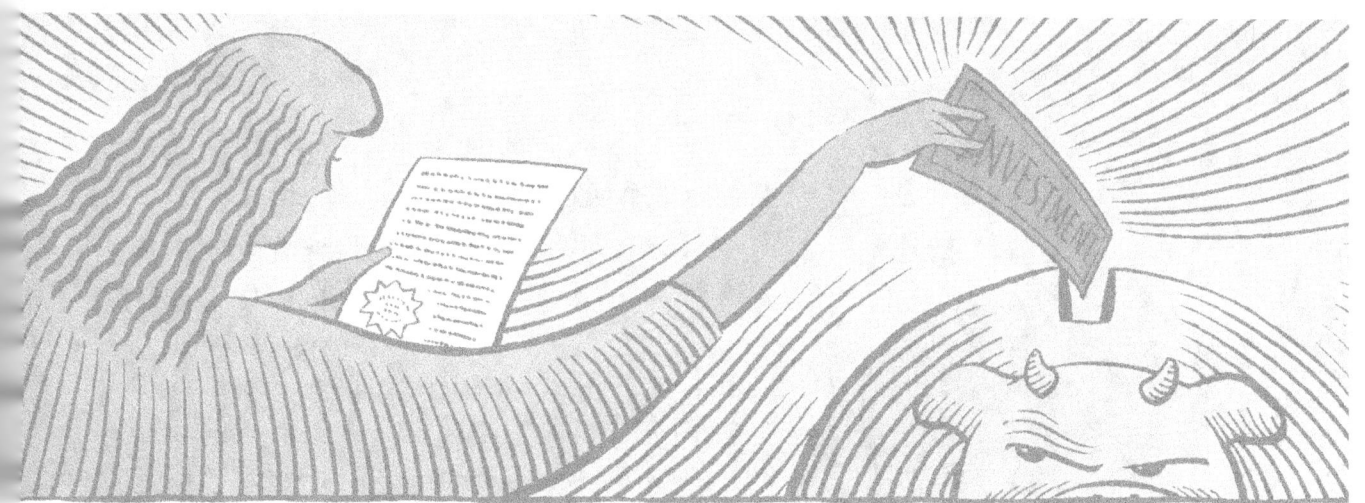

Investment Fraud

Whether they're selling bogus securities, commodities, or oil wells, fraudulent investment promoters try to get you to invest money — lots of it. They will promise you either a large increase in the value of your investment, higher-than-market interest on your capital, or both.

Investment schemers market by mail and by telephone, armed with high-pressure and sophisticated selling techniques. Some swindlers surround themselves with the trappings of legitimacy — rented office space, a receptionist, investment counselors, and professionally designed color brochures describing the investment.

You may be dealing with an investment swindler if you can answer "yes" to the following:

- Does the salesperson make it sound as if you can't lose?
- Are you promised an unusually high rate of return or interest payment on your capital?
- Are you pressured to make a decision because new investment units "are selling fast"?

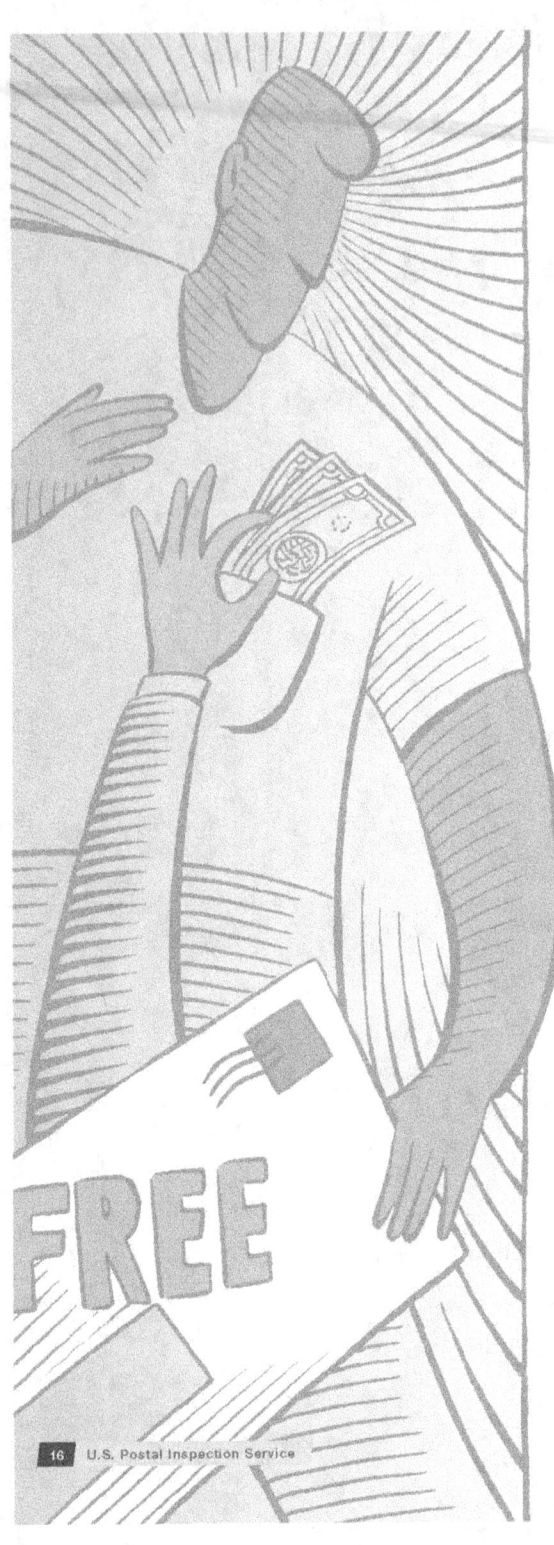

Fees Charged for Normally Free Services

Many services are available free of charge from the government or other organizations. A recent come-on involves offering such services for a fee in the hope that you are unaware the services are available at no cost elsewhere. Beware of mail solicitations that try to get you to pay a fee for such services as:

- Child support collection assistance.
- Unclaimed income tax refunds.
- Property tax exemptions.

Contact the federal, state, and local agencies responsible for these services, and chances are you'll get the information and assistance you need free of charge.

A similar scheme preys on those whose loved ones are missing. If you have missing relatives or friends, be cautious about people who contact you to offer information on the whereabouts of your loved ones for a fee. If you receive such a solicitation, contact law enforcement authorities.

Advance-Fee Loans

Have you had difficulty obtaining a personal or business loan through normal sources? If so, you may become the target of an advance-fee loan scheme, where a con artist offers you a "guaranteed" loan for a fee paid in advance.

The swindler claims to be able to obtain a loan for you with ease from a legitimate lending institution, such as a savings and loan association. However, the swindler has no ability to secure a loan for you. Instead, the swindler steals your fee and either disappears or remains in the area to bilk other unsuspecting victims while stalling you with excuses as to why your loan has not been funded. Protect yourself! Know you're with a legitimate lending institution before entering into a negotiation for any loan, and be certain you understand the terms before you sign on the dotted line.

Business Tip: You may get a letter from a "government official" who offers your company a percentage for its help in secretly transferring millions of dollars from a foreign country. To participate in the lucrative scheme, all you have to do is provide your company's letterhead, invoices, and bank account number. Executives who have fallen for this pitch — which is a complete fabrication — have told horror stories of their losses.

Credit Repair and Credit Card Schemes

Have you been denied a major credit card due to a poor credit rating? Watch out for phony credit repair or credit card offers. Some offers will end up costing you lots of money, and you won't get what you think is being offered.

Scam artists may offer you credit repair services. After paying a large fee, all you receive is a list of banks that offer a secured Visa or MasterCard. "Secured" cards are issued after you deposit enough money to cover any charges you make and are offered by many banks. Save your money and look up these banks in your local Yellow Pages.

Scam artists may also offer a "major credit card" for a fee. But when your card arrives, it can only be used with a specific store or catalog that also happens to be owned by the company that issued your credit card. "Single-use credit cards" are not a new concept, but scam artists misrepresent them as being all-purpose bank credit cards. It can get worse when the merchandise in the catalog from which you must choose your purchases is either inferior or grossly overpriced.

If you have poor credit, be careful when responding to an offer for credit. If you are not satisfied with the information provided in the offer, do not pay any fees up front. Otherwise, you may become a victim.

Work-at-Home Offers

Con artists know that working at home is an attractive alternative for many. That's why they place such ads. Maybe you've even responded to one. Thousands of people have helped unscrupulous promoters pocket victims' hard-earned dollars.

Beware! Work-at-home schemes will not guarantee regular salaried employment. They will require you to invest your money before you learn how a plan works or before you are sent instructions. The work you are asked to do often continues the fraud by getting other victims involved.

The most common type of work-at-home fraud is envelope stuffing. Typically, there is nothing to stuff. Instead, you receive instructions on how to deceive others by placing an ad like the one you responded to! Other schemes require you to assemble gift and specialty products for which there is little or no market.

Always suspect any ad from the mail or via the Internet claiming you can earn unusually high income with little or no effort on your part.

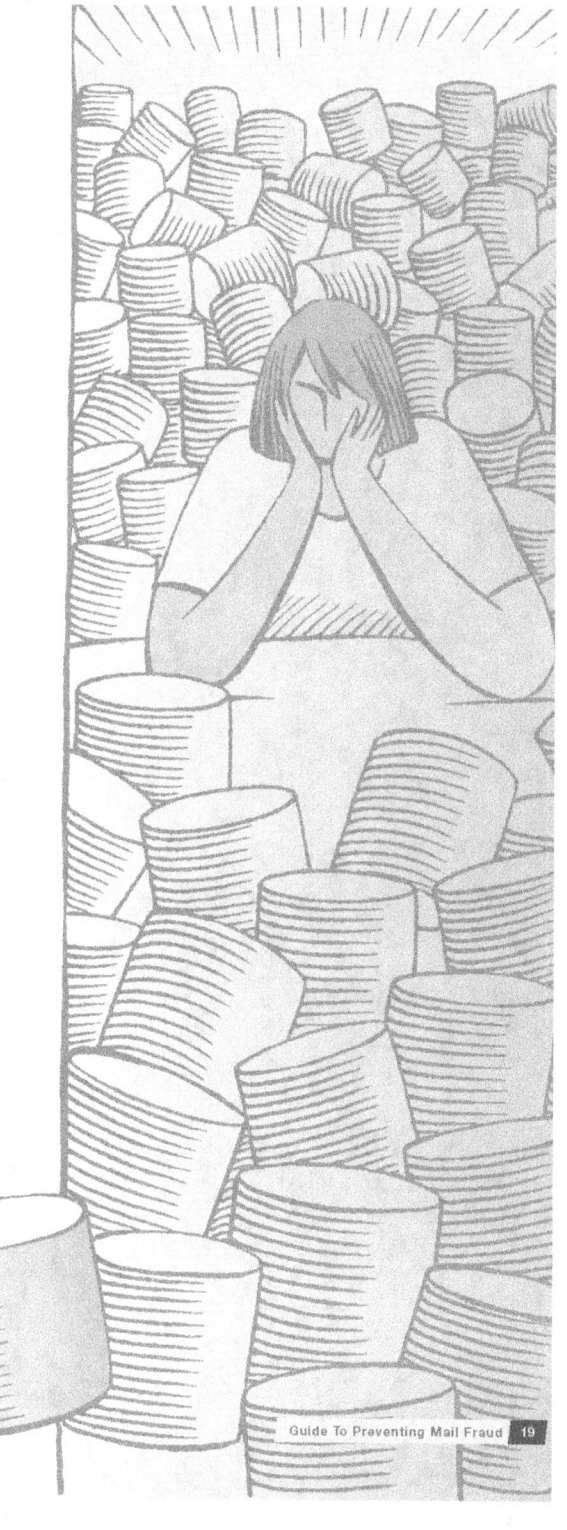

Distributorship and Franchise Fraud

Distributorships and franchises can be legitimate and often profitable forms of business enterprises. Fast food and quick-printing franchises are examples of opportunities offered by national organizations to individuals willing to invest a substantial amount of money for the right to operate such businesses.

Unfortunately, there are some devious promoters who use the cover of legitimate businesses to advertise fraudulent opportunities. They take their investors' money and quietly go out of business.

Watch for these warning signs:

- Promises of unrealistic profits.
- Promoters who seem more interested in selling their distributorship or franchise than they are in the product or service being offered.
- Promoters who are reluctant to let you contact current franchisees.

Phony Job Opportunities

Beware of advertisements that make unbelievable claims about job opportunities. The ads misrepresent wages and the number of jobs actually available, and you must always pay a fee to receive more information. You should beware of job opportunity pitches that:

- Guarantee placement in a job.
- Claim no experience or special skills are needed to qualify.
- Offer too-good-to-be-true wages.
- Offer overseas employment.

Especially be wary of ads that promise to get you a job with the U.S. Postal Service. In return for your money, you may only get generic information that is available free from the Postal Service and from some public libraries. Save your money and contact your nearest Postal Service employment office, or the Postal Service Web site at *usps.com,* to determine if postal jobs are available in your area and to obtain the necessary application forms.

JOB OPPORTUNITIES

Unsolicited Merchandise

A company sends you a gift in the mail — a tie, a good luck charm, or a key chain. You didn't order the gift. What do you do? Many people will feel guilty and pay for the gift. But you don't have to. What you do with the merchandise is entirely up to you.

- If you have not opened the package, mark it "Return to Sender." The Postal Service will send it back at no charge to you.
- If you open the package and don't like what you find, throw it away.
- If you open the package and like what you find, keep it — free. This is a rare instance where "finders, keepers" applies unconditionally.

Whatever you do, don't pay for it — and don't get conned if the sender follows up with a phone call or visit. By law, unsolicited merchandise is yours to keep.

Reshipping Fraud

A relatively new scheme targeting businesses and credit card owners is "reshipping fraud." Criminals operating primarily from Eastern European countries and Nigeria have been conducting widespread, international schemes involving bogus job offers, fraudulent credit card orders, and the reshipping of illegally obtained products.

The scam begins when criminals buy high-dollar merchandise — such as computers, cameras, and other electronics — via the Internet using stolen credit cards. They have the merchandise shipped to addresses in the United States of paid "reshippers" (who may be unaware they are handling stolen goods). The reshippers repackage the merchandise and mail it to locations in Russia, Ukraine, Estonia, Lithuania, Romania, and Germany. Victimized businesses include such well-known companies as Amazon, Gateway, and eBay, and other Internet auction sites.

U.S. Postal Inspectors offer these tips:

- Don't give out personal information to a person or company you don't know.
- Be suspicious of any offer that doesn't pay a regular salary or involves working for an overseas company.
- Check the company with the FTC, Better Business Bureau, or state Attorney General.

Fake Check
Scams

Should you wire money to a stranger? U.S. Postal Inspectors hope you say: Absolutely not! The offer may sound like a nice deal, but — as usual — it's just too good to be true. The check or money order you receive will be counterfeit. And you'll be out the money.

Fake check scams appear in various disguises:

- You're overpaid for an item you sold on the Internet and are asked to wire-transfer back the extra dollars.
- You receive a check with a notice that you've won a foreign lottery or sweepstakes. You're told to deposit the check, representing a portion of your winnings, and wire-transfer $2,000 to $5,000 back "to cover the taxes" so you can collect the rest of your winnings.
- You receive a work-at-home offer that promises, in return for depositing a money order or check to your bank account, you can keep a percentage of the money after wire-transferring the rest.
- Someone in a chat room asks you for a favor: Just cash a check and wire-transfer back the money.
- You see a work-at-home offer online that requires using software to create checks on your computer and mailing the checks to U.S. addresses.

In any case, the check or money order you receive for deposit will be a counterfeit. It will be returned to your bank unpaid, and the full amount will be deducted from your account.

You are responsible for any check or money order you deposit to your account. If the check or money order turns out to be a counterfeit, or is returned unpaid for any reason, you are fully responsible for the loss.

Federal law requires banks to make deposited funds available within 1 to 5 business days. Just because you can withdraw cash from your account soon after depositing a check or money order doesn't mean the item you deposited is valid. It can be weeks before a check or money order is discovered to be a counterfeit and returned to your bank unpaid. Bank employees may not be able to determine whether an item is invalid. Their job is to process your financial document.

How to Contact the U.S. Postal Inspection Service

If you believe you've been victimized by a scam involving the U.S. Mail, you can get help by contacting your nearest Postal Inspection Service office in one of three ways:

1. Call 1-877-876-2455 (press option "4" to report suspected mail fraud).
2. Visit *postalinspectors.uspis.gov* to report suspected fraud online.
3. Mail your queries to this address:

CRIMINAL INVESTIGATIONS SERVICE CENTER
ATTN: MAIL FRAUD
222 S RIVERSIDE PLZ STE 1250
CHICAGO IL 60606-6100

www.ingramcontent.com/pod-product-compliance
Lightning Source LLC
Chambersburg PA
CBHW080802290526
45790CB00008B/3553